Chocolate ICING on Vanilla PROSE

Sandra Glassman

Brilliant Books Literary
137 Forest Park Lane Thomasville
North Carolina 27360 USA

A Lesson Learned

This weary looking cowboy, with a large
brimmed black hat, arrived on the cactus plains
His gun holster loaded, and venom in his veins
Determined this time to end the chore
And do whatever, to even the score
Beads of sweat dripping from his face
Took him twenty years, returning to this
Memory provoking place
Shifting his gaze from left to right
Not a soul, or vulture within sight
Dropping his guard for an instant, to
Quench the thirst, Upon the scene, three
Gun totine men burst, Engulphed by
Fear the cowboy, with the large black hat
Didn't move, stayed still as a cat
For twenty years, wrongly accused, while
Awaiting release, His pent up anger would
Not cease, Now the moment of truth he anticipated
Not from a happening he created,
The three seedy looking sorts, threw down their
Guns and leaped off their horse, The cowboy
Was caught by surprise, Suddenly he didn't wish
Their demise, For back home waiting was his new
Wife, He deemed it no longer necessary
For hatred to ruin his life

A Memory in History

MANY YEARS AGO, DURING OUR NATION'S TURBULENT HISTORY
THERE WAS A TRAGEDY CALLED THE HOLOCAUST
HOW THIS WAS ALLOWED TO OCCUR, IS STILL A DEEP MYSTERYY
PEOPLE TRYING DESPERATELY TO CONCEAL THEIR ENTITIES
HUDDLED MASSES COMING TOGETHER WITHOUT IDENTITIES
THIS HORROR CANNOT BE MEASURED BY ANYTHING BEFORE IT
HOW DID WE ALLOW THE JEWISH PEOPLE TO ENDURE IT?
THE SURVIVORS FACES TELL OF THAT HORRIBLE BLUNDER
BUT THEIR SPIRITS SHOUT BACK LIKE CLAPS OF THUNDER
THINK BACK IF YOU CAN, TO HOW HELPLESS THESE PEOPLE
MUST HAVE FELT
AND TO HOW MANY GRAVESITES THEY MUST HAVE KNELT
PLEASE: I IMPLORE, HAVE COMPASSION FOR YOUR FELLOW MAN
SO SUCH ATROCITIES CAN BE A MEMORY TO FOREVER BAN
LET US REMEMBER, GOD CREATED ALL MEN EQUAL
TO THIS TRAGEDY THERE SHOULD NEVER BE A SEQUEL

A Most Important Win

I PONDER AND SHAKE THE DICE IN MY HAND
CRITICAL DECISION TO BE MADE, CHALLENGE IF I CAN
WHAT TO CHOOSE RED OR BLACK
I ANTICIPATE A PANIC ATTACK
VICTORY IS A MUST IN THE DICE I PUT MY TRUST
CROWDS APPROACH THE GAMING TABLE
MOST WEARING CLOTHING WITH A DESIGNER LABEL
A MIST OF SWEAT FORMS ON MY BROW
MY HANDS DON'T SEEM TO KNOW HOW
TO LET LOOSE THE DICE AND ALLOW
FINALLY MY BET IS PLACED ON THIRTEEN RED
IF I HIT IT RIGHT MY NEXT STOP
WILL BE A HOSPITAL BED
MY HEART HAS BECOME AN ISSUE I NEED A DONOR WITH
COMPATIBLE BLOOD AND TISSUE
THE DICE HAVE COME THROUGH I AM FLUSHED WITH
    ELATION
EVERYTHING HINGED ON THE RIGHT COMBINATION
A WONDERFUL GIFT CAME MY WAY I WILL TREASURE EACH
    DAY

A Plane Tale

YES, THIS IS HEAVEN" A CALL COMES IN
THE ANGEL OPERATOR ON THE OTHER END
CONFIRMS THREE NEW ARRIVALS FOR ENTRANCE
STATE THE CIRCUMSTANCES PLEASE
A SMALL AIRCRAFT HAS PLUNGED INTO THE
DARK NIGHT SEA
THREE PASSENGERS WERE ON BOARD
WITHOUT PARACHUTES OR BALLOON RIPCORDS
PREPARE FOOD AND DRINK
FIX UP THE COTTAGE HAVING THE NUMBER
WRITTEN IN RED INK
THE NEW RESIDENTS ARE NAMED
CAROLYN LAUREN AND JOHN JOHN
IN LIFE THEY ALL EXUDED BEAUTY AND CHARM
THIS TRIO HAD GREAT FAITH AND GAVE OF
THEMSELVES TO AID OTHERS
WE WELCOME THEM TO JOIN OUR FAMILY
OF SISTERS AND BROTHERS
WE IN HEAVEN ARE SO BLESSED
TO HAVE THESE ADDITIONS HERE FOR THEIR
FINAL REST
NO MORE HEARTACHE AND PAIN
FOR HERE IN HEAVEN TEARS FALL AS
SUGAR RAIN AND LAUGHTER IS CANDY CANE

A Poetry Calendar

JANUARY—TIME TO REPLENISH YOUR GOALS
SOMETIMES THAT SEEMS SO DIFFICULT
ALMOST LIKE WALKING ON HOT COALS
THE WEATHER IS DREARY
SO WE FEEL WEARY
SHOVELING THE WHITE CRYSTAL, WE CALL
SNOW
KNOWING IN A FEW MONTHS WE'LL BEGIN
TO HOE
IN CONCLUSION-DEAL WITH JANUARY AS
BEST YOU CAN
FOR THE SUMMER WILL BE HERE IN A
VERY SHORT SPAN

FEBRUARY—IS FOR CUPID OR AFFAIRS OF THE HEART
EMOTIONS RUN STRONG TO KEEP US
HEALTHY AND SMART
WINTER DOLDRUMS CONTINUE TO
SURFACE
THE DAYLIGHT ENDS EARLY
AND PERHAPS OUR MOODS ARE A BIT
SURLY
TAKE PART IN THE SPORTS OF WINTER
AND LOOK FORWARD TO THE WINDS OF
MARCH

MARCH—THE MONTH OF MARCH IS THE TIME TO
        PREPARE
        OUR BACKYARD GARDEN
        WITH NEW SOIL AND SEEDS AND TULIP
        BULBS
        NATURE'S RAIN AND THE BRIGHT SUN
        LIGHT
        WILL CAUSE OUR GARDEN TO GROW AND
        PROSPER
        SOMETIMES THE STRONG WINDS BLOW
        OUR UMBRELLAS
        INSIDE OUT
        WE SEE THE EVIDENCE OF THIS IN THE
        STREET,
        HOPEFULLY THE GUSTY WINDS OF MARCH
        WONT BE TO HARSH

APRIL—APRIL SHOWERS BRING MAY FLOWERS
        APRIL IS ALSO A LOVELY NAME
        APRIL BEGINS THE SEASON OF BASEBALL, ALSO
        THE BEGINNING OF THE GARDEN OVER
        HAUL
        PLANTING AND SEEDING
        BOATING AND WEEDING
        TAXES ARE DUE
        WHAT CAN WE DO
        BUT GRIN AND BARE IT

MAY—COME WHAT MAY
        SOME WILL SAY
        THE MONTH OF MAY IS A PRELUDE TO
        SUMMER
        FLOWERS CONTINUE TO BLOOM, WITH A
        FRAGRANCE
        LIKE PERFUME
        THOUGHTS OF REFACING AND REPLACING

ARE A MUST
SPRING CLEAN UP AND THINGS TO DUST
LOOKING IN THE CLOSETS TO GHOST BUST.
AT THE END OF MAY IS THE MEMORIAL DAY
HOLIDAY
WHEN WE REFLECT ABOUT LOVED ONES
WHO GAVE THEIR
LIVES FOR OUR COUNTRY
THESE HEROS SHOULD BE REMEMBERED
FOREVER

JUNE—THE MONTH OF JUNE IS A MONTH OF SPECIAL
OCCASIONS
AND HAPPY TIMES
GRADUATION AND THE WEDDING SCENE
AND WE HOPE OUR BODIES WILL STAY TRIM
AND LEAN
TO FIT INTO THE WEDDING DRESS THEME
JUNE IS THE END OF THE SCHOOL YEAR
A TIME FOR FRIENDS TO SAY GOODBYE AND
MAYBE SHED A TEAR

JULY—FIREWORKS 4TH OF JULY PARTIES
SWIMMING AND BOATING
BARBECUES AND SUMMER FUN AT THE BEACH
OR POOL
GETTING THE LAWN MOWER READY TO USE
AS A SUMMER TOOL
AIR CONDITIONERS GOING FULL BLAST
WE HOPE THE OPPRESSIVE WEATHER WON'T
LAST

AUGUST—SUMMER DRAWS CLOSER TO THE END
STARTING SCHOOL IS RIGHT AROUND THE
BEND

HAZY DAYS-HUMID NIGHTS
HOPE FOR RAIN ONCE AGAINTO MAKE THE
LAWNS GREENER
BRINGING TO AN END THE SUMMER'S
DELICIOUS WIENERS

SEPTEMBER—FALL BACK TO SCHOOL ROUTINE
CAR POOLS ONCE AGAIN ARETHE SCENE
LEFT OVER MEMORIES OF SUMMER
ROMANCES
AND LOOKING FORWARD TO SCHOOL
DANCES
PARENTS ANXIOUS ABOUT CHILDREN
LEAVING HOME TO
ATTEND COLLEGE
HOPING THAT THEY GAIN A LOT OF
USEFUL KNOWLEDGE

OCTOBER—HALLOWEEN, PUMPKINS MASKS AND GOBLINS
LEAVES TURNING BEAUTIFUL COLORS
ONCE AGAIN COOL ENOUGH TO BAKE
AND RAKE
AND LOOKING FOR OUR DEAR FRIENDS
WE DONT WANT TO FORSAKE

NOVEMBER—THANKSGIVING   DAY   WITH   ALL   THE
TRIMMINGS
CONSUME ALL THE TREATS TODAY AND
WORRY TOMORROW
ABOUT DIET SLIMMING
WEATHER BEGINS TO TURN MUCH
COLDER
PERHAPS BUYING A NEW MEMO
HOLDER

DECEMBER—CHRISTMAS HOLIDAYS
    CHRISTMAS TIME IS HERE
    TIME TO SPREAD GOOD CHEER
    LAUGHTER AND SONG FILL THE NIGHT
    GLISTENING ARE THE STARS
    WAY ABOVE ON HIGH
    LIGHTING UP THE CHRISTMAS TREE
    MEN MADE OF SNOW
    ARE GRINNING AT YOU
    CHESTNUTS AROMAS FILL THE AIR
    COME TAKE MY HAND
    TOGETHER WE WILL STAND
    SHARING OUR FEELING OF GLEE

A Somber Experience

OPENING OF YET ANOTHER HOLOCAUST MUSEUM
PERHAPS THIS ONE WILL HELP ENLIGHTEN THE SKEPTICS
ARRIVING AT THE SCENE
PEOPLE WHO DIDNT BELIEVE
MEMORIES OF LOVES ONES CAN NOW BE RETRIEVED
AS YOU ARRIVE THE ENTRANCE IS BRIGHT
AFTER THE ELEVATOR STOPS AT THE FOURTH FLOOR AND
    THE DOOR OPENS
IT LOOKS LIKE THE DEAD OF NIGHT
CROWDS LEAVE THE ELEVATOR, STANDING AROUND
TO VIEW THIS GRAPHIC EXHIBIT
THEY ARE SOON STUNNED BY THE HORROR
DISPLAYED WITHIN IT
RELATTVES AND STRANGERS VISITTNG TOGETHER
GASPING AT THE REALITY THAT WILL STAY IN
THEIR MIND'S FOREVER
IT SEEMS INCOMPREHENSIBLE THAT ONE MANIACLE MAN
WAS ABLE TO BEGIN THIS PATH OF SORROW AND
DESTRUCTION
THE ANNIHITATION OF RACES, MOSTLY JEWS
KILLED FOR THEIR IDEAS AND DIFFERENT VIEWS
AT THE EXHIBITS END THERE IS A REFLECTING ROOM
WHERE VISITORS CAN THINK ABOUT THE HORROR AND
    GLOOM
BUT AS YOU LEAVE THIS PLACE, ONE CANNOT HELP TO
FEEL A SENSE OF PAIN
BECAUSE HUMAN BEINGS SEEM NOT TO BE ABLE TO
STOP KILLING EACH OTHER OVER AND OVER AGAIN

WHY CANT SOCIETY VIEW VIOLENCE AS SUCHA WASTE
AND THINK ABOUT THE CONSEQUENCES BEFORE
   MAKING
DECISIONS IN HASTE

A Story Poem

The Brown family went for a vacation at their cabin near
Rosemont lake hoping for quiet and seclusion
In the middle of the night while everyone was fast asleep
Brandon Brown who was six heard a loud noise
Tip toeing out of bed he made his way to the kitchen
Peering into the darkened room Brandon saw two grizzley
Black bears! Just at this moment Mom and Dad awoke
Walking slowly towards their son Mom stepped into a
Metal pail causing confusion and soon after the pail shook
Free of her foot hitting her farhead "ouch
Dad scowled making a facial contusion
Pardon the intrusion spoke one of the bears
We were hungry and your cabin was chosen for it's protrusion
And we didn't eliminate it by exclusion
Morning sunlight was drizzling into the cabin by now
Sitting down to breakfast were two bears and the Brown family
As to what happens further on we'll let the reader form their
Own conclusion

A Symphony

To describe a symphony is quite complex
A symphony is harmonious mingling of different sounds
Sounds that can resemble ferocious winds
Sounds like lyrical birds
Sounds of screeching animals when threatened by man
Sounds of softness, sounds of blaring
such is the symphony of the "Grand Canyon"
The north rim has more precipitation, you can hear the
raindrops melody
The south rim of the canyon has silence and solitude
the hot sun gives of the sound of loud trumpets
falling rocks and natures echoes all coming together
Entwined in their awe inspiring grandeur

And So It Goes

And so it goes on the journey of life
Pathetic pairs, obsessive fears, terrified tears, sacrificed cares
Children's shabby teddy bears, money grabbing heirs
Headlights accenting dark eyed reindeers
Switching job gears, society jeers, salesman peddling wares
Truth in court to be sweared, lion cub lairs,
Gray speckled glorious mares, racism's ugly head rears
And so it goes
Reality passing years

Awakenings

Slowly the ice melts upon a gray stone grave
Cold somberness proceeds, and in the distance
a flag briskly waves
Blood, sweat, tears, where have I been for years?
Too busy with everything, not listening to the sound
of my own mind spinning
time is passing fast
no more looking to the past
Too many shadows to erase
Now's the time to create in my own
comfortable space

Big Brother

Can you imagine your life meshed along with ten
People of mixed genders, having no contact with their
Outside big spenders?
Neither T.V. or radio fax machines or cell phones
Camera's following every move and word
For three long months away from family and friends
In the solitude zone
Growing vegetables and picking eggs like living in a co-op
Will these strangers survive without the day to day stress
Power struggles family spats lovers attention?
Setting aside control, opportunity mood swings just to
Shine in a spotlight for money
Society has chosen lust for notoriety and wealth over common sense

Blood

THE RIVER OF BLOOD IS THE TRAIL
BLOOD IS LIFE'S JUICE
BLOOD ISTHE CAROUSEL OF LIVING, HELPING TO KEEP
LIFE FLOWING ALONG WITH OTHER ESSENTIALS
HUMANITY, AS WE KNOW IT, HAS THE COLOR RED
NETWORKING THE FORCE AND PULSE THROUGHOUT
    OUR BODY
AND WHEN WE ARE WOUNDED, WE ALL BLEED THE SAME
    COLOR
WITH THIs IN MIND, FORGET VIOLENCE AND BREED
    KINDNESS
IF ONE AND BLEEDS, WE ALL FEEL THE WOUNDS

Bookends

LIFE IS LIKE BOOKENDS ON THE LIVINGR0OM TABLE
OH! WHAT TALES THEY COULD SPIN
BETWEEN THE COVERS OF EACH NOVEL WHERE DOES
    ONE BEGIN
BIRTH THE CHALLENGING START
IN THE MIDDLE AVOIDING THE INEVITABLE
END, NOT TO DEPART
SOMEWHERE ALONG THE JOURNEYA LIFE TO CHART
MOMENTS OF DECEIT
LAYER UPON LAYER OF LIASIONS INDISCREET
SECRECY AND SILENCE
PROMISES OF DANGEROUS ALLIANCE
CLOSE YOUR EYES, RELAX IN DREAMS
EVERYTHING AND NOTHING IS AS IT SEEMS
REFLECTING BACK, HAPPENINGS PERHAPS COULD
HAVE BEEN REARRANGED
REALISTICALLY, MOST OF THE COURSE CAN'T BE CHANGED

Breathe and Reboot

Breathe and reboot, you've got attitude
Breathe and reboot your no prostitute
Challenges of life's complexity everyday battle with it's simplicity
Dress for job home return to being a slob
Breathe and reboot retool necessary brain function
Take a trip to tuxedo junction
World news global intrigue and local spice
Life's luck of the draw roll the dice
Romantic alliance alluring stay away from focus on boring
Breathe and reboot the spirit within remains forever alive if
Belief in a higher power survives so get jolted with the energy surrounding
Breathe and reboot

Bursting the Bubble

Bubble bubble toil and trouble
An uncomprehensible tragedy has hit at our hearts and
The fabric of humanities existence. Can the horrific
Sights witnessed ever be erased? Will our emotions
Forever carry the burden of this deed? The valiant
Firefighters and medical personal heightened pure
Instinct to be displayed by strangers towards their fellow
Man. Society as we know it is being challenged in a way
Never before.
Red blood was shed and red blood will rebuild with a
Flourish and determination unknown in history.
Grief and valor shall give us more sustainence for a
Triumphant tomorrow

Casual or Suited

The guys and gals in my office each day come attired
In clothing so classy we were greatly admired
Then along came casual Friday dress
What to advise, must I give in to stress
Shopping for snappy yet comfort was a chore
Pastels and kakhi's became a bore
Now with time passed all has goné back
Sharp and spiffy in basic blue and black
Once again our firm know's no bounds
As we send out accountant's to their client rounds

Chant

The sea water wind may blow a spray mist
That casts a reflection on the lake
While the moon shines and glistens upon it
And forms a luminated shadow
A pebble tossed by a child from a creaky wooden
Bridge above causes the water to gently ripple
Into infinity, in the stillness of the moment
One can hear the delicate whispering
"chant" of life

Choices

IT'S NEVER TO LATE, SO THE SAYING GOES
IT'S NEVER TO LATE TO REVERSE THE ROAD YOU CHOSE
SUPPOSEDLY, CHOICES ARE MADE FOR ALL THE RIGHT
  REASONS
BUT AS ONE GROWS OLDER, THE CHANCE FOR CHOICES
PASS MORE QUICKILY THAN THE FOUR SEASONS
HAVING A DREAM EARLY IN LIFE
MAY SOMEHOW CONFLICT WITH YOUR WIFE
YEARS ADVANCE WITH EACH DAY AND THINGS CHANGE
NEVER DISMISS YOUR DREAMS
PERHAPS YOU CAN REARRANGE
IF YOU DESIRE TO BECOME A POET
WRITE DOWN YOUR THOUGHTS, LET EVERYONE KNOW IT
PERCHANCE YOU ASPIRE TO BECOME ARTISTIC
CREATE, DONT DELAY BE REALISTICC
RISE EACH DAY AND GREET A NEW DAWN
HAPPINESS CAN DRIFT IN, SO DONT BE WITHDRAWN
FACE EACH CHALLENGE HEAD ON WITHOUT A MOAN
AND YOULL INCREASE YOUR CHANCE TO
"ROMANCE THE STONE"

Coming Together

CAN THE HUMAN RACE RESIDE TOGETHER
IN HARMONY AND PEACE
RESTRAINING VOCAL TIRADES
NO LONGER ALLOWING ANGER
AND IMPATIENCE TO RULE
CHARITY AND COMPASSION, SHARING
KNOWLEDGE AND ACCUMULATED POSSESSIONS
WITH OUR FELLOW MAN
DISCARDING UNNEEDED CLUTTER
PERHAPS FOR SOMEONE A WANTED TREASURE
SHARING QUALITY TIME WITH A LONG WALK
SIDE BY SIDE FOR A CHATTED TALK
IF FUTURE SOCIETY CAN NOT BRIDGE THEIR
DIFFERENCES, THERE WILL BE NO FUTURE
AS WE KNOW IT

Computer Date

Seated in the office I watched as the computer spit out
Her picture I was mesmerized at first glance
The dating service implied she was ready for a new romance
We continued through e-mail to converse a meeting date
Printout was dispersed I approached my clothes closet
Anxious to find the right stuff Not to nerdy REAL BUFF
Finally clothed and smelling great I was ready to meet my date
Her computer image so pretty strained my brain I hoped she would be
     friendly not vain
Entering the cafe where the meeting was to take place I saw
Her seated in a corner space striding at a fast pace I stopped
In front of her lovely face
From then on the evening floated by we had alot in common
The evening night became the morning sky
Seeing this we left in a hurry both of us to our jobs we did scurry
We made a promise to meet again very soon
By the light of a silvery moon

Coping with Winter

IT's WINTER
THE LANDSCAPE GIVES IT AWAY
TREES AND BUSHES STILLED FROM MOVEMENT
DUE TO THE ICE THAT's FORMED FROM THE FRIGID
    TEMPERATURE
ICICLES, SHARP AS DAGGERS HANG FROM CARS. PORCHES.
AND OUR EYELASHES
EVEN THE BRIGHT SUNSHINE DOESN'T MELT THE ICE
    BELOW OUR FEET
WALKING IS LIKE NAVIGATING A MINE FIELD
RIDING BY INTHE CAROUR FACES PRESSED AGAINST THE
    WINDOW
WE CAN SEE SLEDS WITH CHILDREN ABOARD
THEIR FACES CHILLED AND ROSY FROM THE BLUSTERY
    WINDS
IF WE'RE LUCKY WE CAN STOP FROM OUR TRAVELS
TO ENTER A QUAINT CAFE
THE SMELL OF FRESH BREWED COFFEE FILLS OUR
    NOSTRILS
HOW LOVELY THESE WINTER DAYS WITHTHIS EXQUISITE
    SCENERY ARE UNTIL THE LAST THAW
THEN WINTER'S LANDSCAPE IS GONE ONCE MORE

Couch – Pouch

LUMPY, AND VERY BUMPY IS MY STRIPED RED COUCH
PRETZELS, POPCORN MOVIE VIDEO, UPON THE WORN
GLASS COFFEE TABLE, ALONG WITH MY TIRED FEET
NESTLING IN MY FAVORITE COMFORTABLE TORN SLIPPERS
LUMPY, BUMPY IS MY TEE SHIRT ATTEMPTING TO COVER
THE OVER FORTY MID SECTION
SITTING DOWN WANTING ONLY PRIVACY AFTER A HARD
DAYS WORK MY ONE DESIRE IS TO CLICK ON THE VCR
LOAD THE MOVIE AND MUNCH ON THE ASSORTED
    CRUNCHIES
NO SUCH LUCK* * *JUST AS THE FIRST SUCTION OF
    BUTTERED
POPCORN ENTERS MY AWAITING LIPS THE LITTLE WIFE
    SETS
HERSELF ALONG SIDE, SNUGGLES UP TO ME AND SAYS
"I'M SO GLAD YOUR HOME THE SINK DRAIN IS CLOGGED"
SO MUCH FOR A QUIET COUCH POUCH NIGHT

Current Politics

Mr. and Mrs. White House
For the first term of four young and vigorous
Early on fashionably hip, glowing expression
Smiles abundant soon turning to stale stares
What caused all this change, Mr. and Mrs president
Intelligent, yet accepting strategy advised
By some not so wise
Having to explain consequences of immature behavior
Judgment majorly impaired, scandal hinted
Use of language verbally dissected turning words
Into a linguistic puzzle, life's achievements
Threatened for a few passionate moments
Mr. and Mrs. White house what will the future be?
A extremely popular president, perhaps having
To retreat like a general falling on his sword

Poem – Daily Life

The earth revolves on its axis
Harried people pay their taxes
Everyone so completely absorbed
Look to the beauty of living and
       don't be bored
Death and taxes are a part of life
So try not to let it add to the
    misery and strife
When things cannot change, try to
     rearrange your hopes
   and dreams and lust for life

Day Dreams

THE DARKNESS OF THE EVENING
THE STILLNESS OF THE MOON
AND AS THE SUN RISES, YET ANOTHER MORNING
    AWAITS US
IN THE HOT HUMID MONTH OF JUNE
THE FRAGRANCES OF RASPBERRY AND LILAC, TINGLE OUR
    SENSATION
OF SMELL
SUMMER BARBECUES AND FIREWORKS GIVE US THE
    CHANCE TO YELL
ON A LINGERING SUMMER DAY, WE MIGHT DREAM OF A
    WISHING WELL
WHILE RECITING EXPERIENCES WE WANT TO TELL

Decisions

The eagle, a bird of prey
Longingly looks around and thinks
what will dine on today
the precision of the eagle as the mouse
lies in wait
will the eagle swoop down or will the mouse
be eagle bait
the eagle stares, his eyes pierce
the eagle decides, the mouse is wise
He leaps aside, let's the eagle collide with the
empty space in the ground
will the eagle have dinner at eight?
or will the mouse be long gone from his plate

Descriptions

Indigo moon sapphire sky
White marshmallow clouds
Casually drift by
Blind sighted by black
Icicles glowing silver gray
Children riding bicycles enjoying
A new day
Lemon yellow roses white chocolate
From the alps red licorice sticks
Kiss from a spouse
Concert grand piano starched white blouse
Novel of dark mystery injustices during
Our history
When all is said and done
The written word can stir the heart
Like the exquisite setting of a sun

Enlighten to Brighten

Imagine if the human brain were made of glass
Would there be a difference between a lad and lass
Does to see dearly mean to accept? or will fear of the
Unknown cause one to object, no layer covering to taint
The prejudicial skin paint heart, lungs, facial expression
No need for mankind aggression
The world can be so beautiful, nature's change of seasons
Everything has it's reason
Power in the wrong hands can produce evil, causing
Terrible upheaval, take a long hard glance
As the morning sun beams for another day
Share a kind word or gesture
That should be the human way

Expression

SEE ME AS I AM, NOT AS YOU PERCETVE ME TO BE
DON'T CLOSE YOUR EYES, TO THE PROMISE OF A NEW
   TOMORROW
TENDERNESS IS EVERYTHING
EVEN A DREAM CAN AWAKEN THE MIND
SINCEREITY CAN CLAIM TO BE MAGIC, BUT
KILL TIME, DONT REVEL IN THE SECURITY OF IT
SECRETS CAN'T DIMINISH LOVES POWER
NEVER BE AFRAID TO EXPRESS YOURSELF
FOR THAT CAN BE THE SALVATION OF YOUR
COURAGE

Flowers

Petals of the fragile flowers swiftly and
quietly rebound to the fertile grass
Green, so green are the trees in the
pre-summer bloom
Iridescent colored floral bouquets growing
in groups line the front of homes
Purple rhododendrons, white and pink
cherry blossoms, and multi-colored
marigolds
Rising from the earth, to be cleansed
with the cooling rains of spring and
embraced by the glow of the hot
summer sun

Goodbyes

Never say goodbye in anger
never say so long in haste
Don't treat time as a given thing
Because time is too precious to waste
never quarrel for superficial reasons
your regrets can't cover all the seasons
grown up maturity is truly an endeavor
However, saying goodbye may be forever and ever

Heaven Above

IS THERE A VACANCY IN HEAVEN?
ONLY THE LANDLORD, CAN KNOW FROM HIGH ABOVE
IS THERE A PLACE IN HEAVEN
FOR ANGELS, WHICH SIGNIFY PEACE AND LOVE
WHY ARE THE CHOSEN SELECTED
WHAT CAN BE THE RENT
DOES ONE HAVE TO LIVE A LIFE OF
MATERIAL DENIAL
AND THE FORTHRIGHTNESS TO REPENT
SO MANY BRIDGES TO BURN
SO MANY SPACES TO OCCUPY
WHY DO THE GOOD DIE YOUNG?
I MUST QUESTION WHY
IS THERE A VACANCY IN HEAVEN?
ONLY TIME WILL TELL
IF BEING GOOD AND KIND
WILL PAY OFF AS WELL
I IMAGINE SPACE IN HEAVEN IS WANTED
BY ALL
BUT, I BELIEVE ONLY THE LANDLORD
IN HEAVEN CAN MAKE THAT IMPORTANT CALL

Identity

I FEEL LIKE A BIRD THAT'S FALLEN
AND CAN'T FIND IT'S WAY
SO FRAGILE IS MY SPIRIT
THAT I'M TEMPTED TO PRAY
I HAVE NO IDENTTTY WITHOUT MY FAMILY TIES
MY FACE IS HAPPY, BUT MY HEART KNOWS THAT'S A LIE
LIFE IS SO COMPLEX, I CAN ONLY ACCEPT REALITY IF I PRETEND
BUT ONCE PEACE COMES, I'LL BE ABLE TO MEND

Inner Strength

There may come a time in our all to
secure day
When a jolt from above makes us eager
to pray
no one can predict for sure when our
inner strength will be put to a
test
so let us always hope for the best
Keep in mind a positive thought
Cheer yourself with something that's
bought
Turn your thoughts to others, They
may give you a clue
But most of all keep hope alive and
never fell blue

Innocence

WHAT CONSTITUTES INNOCENCE
DOES IT COMMENCE WITH BIRTH, AND THROUGH
   LIFE'S
EXPERIENCE BECOME LOST
CAN ONE'S THOUGHTS AND FEELINGS SOMEHOW
   COVER
UP GUILT SO ONE IS NAIVE?
AT BIRTH THE MIND IS FREE
ONLY FROM THE PROCESS OF LIFE DO WE BECOME
TAINTED
SILENCEIS NEVER GOLDEN INTHE FACE OF INJUSTICE

Invisible Carousel

Does to view equal reality? can the brain distinguish beauty
From banality? contusions, illusions, on a merry-go-round
Of frivolity, jocularity laughter, smiles children seated on
Carved animal creatures moving up and down to loud
Carnival tunes, these painted animals having diverse
Facial symmetry appearing almost alive
Adults on the sidelines shoutng
"Reach FOR THE BRASS RING"
As if such an accomplishment could insure continued
Happiness, the invisible carousel of life revolving
Spinning, like out of touch characters from stories of old
Not in sequence with reality
Giving in to banality
Completly devoids gallantry
Thus becomes finality

Invisible Chains

DON'T BE SURROUNDED BY INVISIBLE CHAINS
TO RESTRICTING, CAN'T CHANGE LANES
RESTRAINING THOUGH THEY MAY BECOME
IT'S UP TO YOU TO KNOWW WHERE THERE COMING
    FROM
BREAK THE TIES,
THAT WILL SET YOU FREE
CLEAR YOUR CONSCIOUS AND THEN YOU WILL BEGIN TO
    SEE
THE ONLY CHAINS THAT SEEM TO BIND
ARE THE INVISIBLE CHAINS OF THE MIND

Island In Danger

Bubble, Bubble, Double Trouble
Firey Red Embers, Smoldering
Ground, Oozing Volcanic Eruption
Nature's Cremation of the Earth
Charred Matter Overtaking This
Beautiful Island Paradise
Monserat, a Wondrous Embodiment
Of Tranquil Water, Foliage, Island
Population Obscured From Lifes
Stressing Pace, Now Forced To
Vacate From Their Life And
Livelyhood Unsure of the Future
As Nature Unleashes It's Rath
There Are No Boundaries

I Wish I Knew

WHAT DOES IT TAKE TO BE BRAVE
I WISH I KNEW
FOR SOME IT'S FACING LIFE EVERYDAY
AND SOMEHOW MANAGING NOT TO FEEL BLUE
OTHERS FACE THE HIGHEST OBSTACLES WITH
    COURAGE IN THEIR HEARTT
EVEN IF THE WINDS OF DESPAIR BLOW RIGHT
THROUGH AND STING LIKE
    A DART
SOME OF THE HUMAN RACE CAN ACCEPT THE EVER
    EVOLVING CHANGES,
        AND NOT QUESTION WHY
COUNTLESS OTHERS REFUSE TO EVEN TRY
WITH EACH PASSING SUNRISE THAT WILL INEVITABLY
    BECOME THE NIGHT
PERHAPS WE ARE ONE OF THE LUCKY ONES, TO HAVE
    A LOVED ONE WHO
CAN SHARE OUR FEARS AND HOLD US CLOSE AND
    TIGHT
THE MYSTERY THAT IS LIFE REMAINS
EACH OF US COPING IN OUR OWN WAYY
WHY DES THE BELIEF IN A HIGHER POWER GIVE
    SUCH COMFORT
I WISH I KNEW

Journeys

Life's road is like a brief dramatic skit
it seems so short when you reflect upon it
The most fascinating of life's lessons aren't taught
and the real joy of life is nothing store bought
it's having someone to love
loves rewards cannot be compared
for all the good times you shared
feeling so much love in your heart
being so blue when you're apart
all of these emotions are enclosed
with words that you chose
Don't let love slide by trying to hide
your true thoughts with false pride
say what you have to say today
Before the love of your life slips away

Labor Of Love

A DOLLOP OF COLORFUL CLAY
MOLDED INTO A DESIGN OF BEAUTY
TWISTED AND SWOLLEN FINGERS
EXHIBITING THEIR TOLL FROM THE
TIME CONSUMING POUNDING
WITH CAREFUL HESITATION AND THOUGHT
WHAT CAN BE THE RESULT
ALAS! GIFTED ARTIST HARD AT WORK
BRINGING FORTH THE FRUITS OF HIS LABOR
BEAUTIFUL ROSES, POETRY WITH HANDS

Learning Knowledge

They sit in the classroom
Some with blank faces
The students there are from all different races
at the head of the room
the person who will assume
the responsibility of lifting the gloom
can it be possible to achieve such a task
for this person to somehow bask
and inspire the class to react to
getting their education
Because knowledge is the key for
the future of our nation
Let us respect the persons who teach
for that is the best way they can reach
the thirst for learning is always there
so the teacher is the key to making us aware

Listening Pleasure

The genius of composers from days long past
Is the reason their musical miracles last and last
Beethoven, Handel, Mozart and Bach excerpts and themes from old
Masterpieces can be found in current music which our culture calls
Pop rock, if anyone listens with a keen ear they will realize why the
Beauty of classical music endures year after year
Sit back and set in a compact disc, proceed to listen there is no risk
Stacotto, trills and grace notes are as intriguing and timely as
      Beautiful
Quotes bursting forth these vibrant sounds of music can bring an
      aura
Of thrills along with this comes a feeling of spine tingling chills
      certain
Instruments mimic a marching toy solider
Other combined instruments such as a harp can produce the feeling
Of a delicate butterfly on the shoulder, cymbols clanging silver
Triangle dangling bass drum banging fingers tinkling on the ivory
      keys
Rustling winds through the trees ballerina's turning toe whirls
Conductor using pointer hand twirls
All in all listening is such a treat
I imagine i'm the one whose the keeper of the beat

Liquid Grace

ABOVE CRYSTAL CLEAR RED SUNSET
SLOWLY DIMINISHING FROM THE SKY
ALMOST INTO THE RIM OF THE OCEAN
WATER CREATURES OF DIVERSE SIZE AND SHAPES
TWIRLING AND WHIRLING AS THEY SCAVENGE FOR
FOOD ESSENTIAL TO SURVIVE IN THEIR VAST HOME
SUDDENLY THE SUBMARINE BELOW IS CRIPPLED
BY AN UNEXPECTED EXPLOSION INSIDE SLOWLY
THE SAILORS ABOARD WILL LOSE OXYGEN AND
BREATHING WILL CEASE UNLESS A MIRACLE OCCURS
RESCUE MISSIONS WILL TRY TO SAVE THESE BRAVE
MEN THE TASK RISKY AND DANGEROUS
PAINFULLY NOT A MURMUR OR WHISPER IS HEARD
THE LIQUID GRACE OF THE OCEAN WILL BE MARRED
FOREVER

Lovely Autumn

IN AUTUMN TREE'S BECOME SLOWLY UNCLOTHED
SEASON OF PUMPKIN PICKING, LAWNS DECORATED
WITH
SCARECROWS, HOT APPLE PIE, GOBLINS AND GHOSTS
FOOTBALL GOAL POSTS
UP TO THE ATTIC WARM SWEATERS NEEDED NOW
HOLIDAY SEASON APPROACHING
LOTS TO DO * * *AND HOW* * *
PREPARE FOR THE CHILLY SHIVERING DAYS
FROST AND SNOW CHECK CAR AND TIRES READY TO
GO
SQUIRRELS GATHERING FOOD FOR THEIR FAMILY
MEAL
CRISP FALL AIR MAKES DOING CHORES EASY WITH ZEAL
TOASTING MARSHMALLOWS AROUND A FIELD FIRE
AFTER
A SOCCER GAME
AUTUMN CAN ALSO BE DESCRIBED AS GETTING ON IN
YEARS
AGE IS HOW YOU FEEL DON'T SHED TEARS
THE LOSE OF AN HOUR BY SETTING CLOCKS TO CLIMB
CAN'T DIMINISH THE ELEGANT, ARTISTIC SCULPTURE
OF AUTUMN TIME

Lyrical Love

WHO CHARMS THE THUNDEROUS ROAR FROM THE
   SKY
WHO CAN COAX THE BIRDS TO SING SO YRICALLY AS
   THEY
FLY BY
WHO IS ALWAYS SO CARING, AND GENTLE AS EACH DAY
   PASSES BY
WHO IS THERE TO SUPPORT THE FAMILY AND GIVE SO
   FREELY TO
OTHERS AND NEVER QUESTIONS WHY
WHOSE IS THE SOOTHING HAND TO WIPE TEARS IF I CRY
WHO KNOWS WHAT TO SAY THE TIMES I BREATHE A
   HEAVY SIGH
IT'S YOU MY LOVE
AND BECAUSE OF THESE THINGS MY LIFE IS A
   CONSTANT HIGH

Memorial Day

The cold gray dawn blares down on the white headstones
Here they reside, some heros some not
But they have something in common
They were shot!
These brave people gave of their lives and heeded the
call
Knowing full well it wasn't going to be a ball
Now as you view these loved ones on another
"Memorial Day"
We as your family stand proudly tall
Hopefully you made this nation safer for one and all

Mind Games?

I met a stranger I know I did
The cruise brochure promised romance
And romance I encountered
He had the most expressive round brown
Coffee bean eyes so inticing and yet sensitive
Meeting him made my first venture since
Becoming widowed a dream come true
The cruise sightseeing was dull in comparision
This mystery man payed attention only to me
His demeanor enchanted my being I became
Blinded by infatuation, The cruise ended
Passengers disembarked, he vanished
Did rough seas or some unknown ailment
Play tricks on my brain,? Was it mind games?

No Time to Die

TIME WAITS FOR KNOW ONE
IT PASSES YOU BY
BUT TAKING CHARGE OF YOUR LIFE
AND FILLING IT WITH LAUGHTER AND SONG
LEAVES YOU NO TIME TO DIE
MAKING THE MOST OF THE GIVEN DAY
ACTING ON YOUR INSTINCTSS
AND DOING WHAT YOU SAY
TAKE HOLD OF EVERY OPPORTUNITY
LET YOUR SPIRIT SOAR FREE
EVERY NOW AND THEN TEARS MIGHT APPEAR
WHEN SOMETHING SAD OCCURS
HELPING OTHERS WHO NEED OUR CARE
MAY OVERCOME A HIDDEN FEAR
NEVER BE AFRAID OF LAUGHTER
A SENSE OF HUMOR IS THE KEY TO LIFE
WITH THIS IN MIND YOU CANT GO WRONG
JOIN THE HUMOR WITH A SONG
THEN THERE WILL BE NO TIME TO DIE

Observations

Long ago as legends tell
stories were told about the wishing well
sonnets and ballads were verbally sneered
while cherubs and lilacs were
beautifully cared
Musicians, Artists were heralded by fame
while writers and poets were acknowledged quite tame
and so it goes in the picture framed
by life
true genius sometimes borne of
misery and strife

One Great Day

Buses Arriving, People Disembark
Carrying Luggage, Prepared to be a card shark
Some rushing to play the slot machines
Serious intent, not a lark
Standing at the shiny glittering slot machines
Tossing in money, hoping for
To bring home for my honey
Hour after hour, making gains and loss
My inner voice telling me "Go for the big stakes"
Don't gather any moss, debating I switch my M.O.
Off to the poker table I go
Placing my bet on red number ten
Starting to win, again and again
Just then over the loud speaker I hear a voice saying
Time for the return trip, all the way home I want to flip
At the door my honey is waiting for me
I try to hide my obvious glee

Our Individual Moniker

WHAT'S IN A NAME? CAN'T BE ALL GOOD OR BAD
WON'T PROMISE ONE FAME, MIGHT RENDER YOU SAD
LAUGHTER MAY BE A BY PRODUCT
IF THE SYLLABLES JUST DONT FLOW
A FLOWER BY ANY OTHER NAME
FRAGRANCE FREE, NO PETALS TO SHOW
NICKNAMES, STAGE NAMES, DESIGNATED MONIKER
SOME DIFFICULT TO PRONOUNCE
AS WITH THE HOLIDAY HANUKAH
ACCOMPANYING US THROUGHOUT LIFE
CHANGED FOR A WOMEN, TAKING ON THE ROLE OF
WIFE
DISLIKE THE IDENTIFYING MARKER YOU WERE GIVIN
NO SWEAT!!! CHANGE IT, WHILE YOU ARE STILL LIVIN
FIRST AND FOREMOST, EACH ONE OF US IS UNIQUE
DON'T RAISE AN EYEBROW, IF SOMEONE MAKES A
REMARK
EVERYONE TRIES TO OFFER UNWANTED CRITIQUE

Prozac and Poetry

THE RELATIONSHIP OF PROZAC AND POETRY MAY
    SEEM
TO MAKE ONE FEEL DELIRIOUS
BUT THE REALITY OF IT CAN SEEM QUITE SERIOUS
POETRY CAN ENHANCE THE MIND
PROZAC RELEASES THE CHAINS THAT BIND
THE MIND WORKS IN WAYS THAT AREA MYSTERY
POEMS HAVE BEEN THE SALVATION TO MANY
    THROUGHOUT HISTORY
INSTEAD OF RELYING ON ARTIFICIAL SOURCES FOR
    TRANQUILITY
USE YOUR OWN GIVEN RESOURCES TO THE BEST OF
    YOUR ABILITY

Pump and Grind

Sunlight peeking through the window
Brain barely awake eyes wide shut
Leave bed to look in mirror
Flexing facial muscles
Toothpaste pump dispenser ready
Oozing striped glop for cleaning teeth
Exercise regiment started, proceed to kitchen
Cabinet for coffee to grind pour aromatic beans
Into grinder and "Viola" coffee
Pumper for the heart to begin a day
Onward to shower lather with soap in a pump
Completely attired now ready for work
Reality check no gas in auto Oh well self service
Pump awaits me, a few quick moves
On my way to another day in "Paradise"

Quotes of Nature

ODE TO THE RAINDROPS
BALLAD FOR THE ROSE
REQUIEM MASTERS THE
THUNDERSTORM
OPUS SCORES THE TIDALWAVES
LULLABYE TUNES SERENADE LILACS
OPERATIC CRESCENDO AS THE
EARTHQUAKE TREMORS
PRELUDE SPRINGS THE EDELWEISS
MINUET MANUEVERS MARIGOLDS
SONATA TO THE SUN RISE
MAN REAPS WHAT HE SOWS
HUMANITY TO ONE ANOTHER WILL
GENTLY ALTER MAN'S WOES

Reality

THE MELLOW YELLOW CHERUBIC SMILE OF THE SUN
THE IMPRESSIONS OF FOOTPRINTS IN THE DEWY GRASS
      AS ANOTHER DAY HAS BEGUN
AT NOON TIME WE'RE ANXIOUS FOR THAT HOT
    DOG ON A BUN
JUST ABOUT FIVE O'CLOCK WE ARE ON THE
    HOMEBOUND RUN
SUDDENLY OUT OF THE BLUE SOMEONE'S VOICE IS
    STILLED
    BY ANOTHER LOADED GUN
REALITY!
WHAT'S HAPPENED TO LIFE'S FUN?

Reality Pits

CHANGES, EVER SO GRADUAL CHANGES FROM PLATINUM
BLOND TO DRAB GRAY TO SLOWING DOWN FROM THE
THINGS WE DO EVERY
    DAY
THE WEATHER EFFECTS THE BONES
NO MORE ENJOYING ICE CREAM CONES
SOMETIMES FORGETTING THE MOST IMPORTANT
    THINGS
LIKE FACES IN THE MIRROR, REFLECTING OUR MOOD
    SWINGS
IT SEEMS THE JOURNEY HAD JUST BEGUN
AND NOW THE YEARS BEGIN AND END, WITH LESS
    FUN
I SUPPOSE THAT'S HOW LIFE IS MEANT TO BE
SO JUMP AT EVERY CHANCE YOU HAVE FOR THE
    BEAUTY OF LIFE
EVERYONE KNOWS ABOUT REALITY!

Relationships to Fabric

STURDY-DURABLE-LOVINGLY ADORMENT
BOTH CAN BE SMOOTH OR TORN APART
CHOICES MAY NOT BE WISE OR SMART
FEELINGS-TOUCH-SENSITIVITY TO DETAILS
CAREFUL INTRICATE STITCHING DELIGHTFUL TO
    BEHOLD
SEE THROUGH LACE EMPTY TALKING SPACE
ROUGH AROUND THE EDGES
CAN SAVE FROM JUMPING OFF BUILDING LEDGES
FUZZY TO PROVIDE WARMTH FROM WITHIN
LOOKING GLASS SHEER-THIN SKINNED
NEVER UNDER ESTIMATE THE OBVIOUS
IT CAN BE STARING YOU IN THE FACE

Risking It All

I gaze up and see
My name in bright lights on the marquee
I have star billing
Wishing for this so despartely didn't make me smile
Leaving behind my lover, my friend my guy
Promising to return the bridges yet to burn
Must I skip the fame, no pain no gain
Broadway's no place for love, no place for happiness
Fame isn't cozy or warm I'll take fuzzy slippers and a kiss
Down the romantic isle of bliss
Do I have to risk it all? forgo my lifelong dream
All for the sake of love.

Seasonal Changes

Seasons continue their cycle of life
Each of us hoping for less stress and strife
Winter comes with falling flakes of snow
Bring along the sunblock to the beach
To avoid the burn from the summer sun glow
Droplets of moisture as the autumn winds doth blow
Drown out the shrill sounds of a black crow
A quiet on the lake row
Nature's ever growing grass to mow
On a crisp windy day watching mother duck

Striding across the street with seven babies in tow
Every season has its high and low
Keep a positive karma for life's status quo from woe

Self Worth

Games people play
continue everyday
from keeping a stray dog at bay
while pretending to pray
continuing to work
grumbling about being a clerk
middle of the morns coffee clutch
people huddling to speak in a whispered hush
riding home in fancy cars
after drinking in the bars
knowing that's like suicide
to drink and drive perchance to collide
fragile promises never kept
to false tears that have just wept
don't exist to be a number
think before committing that blunder

Silent Beauty

Crypt of angular dimension, artistically
Imaginative and romantic
Oval ellipic, spiral gated entombment of life's
Past mystery, concealed secrets, unknown
Identity shrouded in black velvet
No visitors allowed, quiescent at rest
Unguarded yet safely hidden
A night darkened by the moon
Drenched by the rain
Kissed at dawn by sunlight

Sky above Land Below

Darkness and gloom loom large before the droplets
Mortals kneel to the sky and pray
Alluring multicolored half circles appear after
Ancient civilizations pound drums and dance in groups
In hopes that the rythymic pulsations could provide salvation
From starvation
The rains of springtime help to grow food for many
The grass and trees are clothed by the beauty of nature

Snow

IN THE EVENING OF A MOONLIT NIGHT
THE SNOW TRICKLES DOWN FROM THE SKY
EACH FLAKE A BEAUTIFUL SHAPE
THE SNOW IS WHITE, THE SNOW IS BRIGHT
IT LINGERS ON THE CARS AT NIGHT
IN THE WINTERS TWILIGHT GLOW
FOOTSTEPS SHUFFLE TOO AND FRO
ON OUR FACES THE SNOW FEELS LIKE CRYSTAL CANDY
WE TAKE FOR GRANTED NATURES WONDERS
BUT ALONG WITH THE BEAUTIFUL, COMES NATURES
BLUNDERS
IT IS IMPOSSIBLE TO PREDICT THE FUTURE
SO WHY NOT TREASURE EACH OF LIFE'S SIMPLE
PLEASURES

Society – Violets

VIOLETS AND ROSES
OUTSIDE GARDEN HOSES
KEEPING UP WITH MR. AND MRS JONES
CHOCLATE ICE CREAM DRPPING CONES
HARD BODIES IN FRONT OF MIRROR
PUMPING UP MUSCLE TONES
BANKS HELPING TO GIVE LOANS
STOMPING ON THE FEELINGS OF OTHERS
TO HELP JUSTIFY WHAT WE'VE SOWN
IS IT WORTH IT JUST TO KEEP SALVATION
OUR OWN?

Societys Rhythm

Through a progression of a specific beat
Our life goes along pulsating with heat
from the neighborhood slum, to the everyday hum-drum
along with this can come a spark
Even though it may be just a shot in the dark
the worker outdoors, even if it pours
keeps the beat with his jack hammer
pounding out the sound so loud
but at the end of his day, so proud
the musician in the subway station
drumming his beat for money and elation
the cop also walks to a beat eyeing people in the street
the doctor with his stethoscope
listening and giving his patients hope
little children playing ball
pound, pound laughing at it all
white coffee pot family staples
Beats to a rhythm before coming to the table
Inevitably all beats must come to an end
so let society be willing to bend and lend a hand
if it's outreaching and practice what we've been preaching

Sounds

THE TRILLING OF A WHIPPOURWILL
THE TRANQUIL SILENT SEA
CRUNCHING OF A SHOE AS IT LEAVES IMPRINTS IN THE
    SNOW
THE CLIPPING NOISE OF THE TREE'S BRANCHES
    AS THEY FALL BELOW
CLAPS OF THUNDER FROM A SUMMER STORM
THE BRIGHT YELLOW BLARE OF THE SUN
NONE OF THESE SOUNDS CAN BE AS BEAUTIFUL
AS THE DIALOGUE OF MUSIC WHICH CAN BE ENJOYED
    BY EVERYONE

Space Adventure

My space vehicle landed, quick as could be the
Crew disbanded afraid and alone in outer space
My brain did a flip, flop race suddenly there was
A gentle knuckle rap on the space ship door
I hustled myself quickly to the floor
Peering out from behind a safe place
An evil eyeball was staring in my face
Beads of sweat formed on my suit of space
I reached into the pocket hoping it still contained
The vile of mace just then I heard a voice
I realized there was a choice standing over me
Was my wife screaming I had been asleep
And dreaming about out of space beaming
The time passed was only one hour
I slowly got dressed for work, but not before
Stepping into a very hot shower

Spiritual Love

OUT OF THE DARKNESS INTO THE NIGHT
OUT OF THE SHADOWS YOU ARE MY GUIDING LIGHT
THE HURRICANE OF LIFE TWISTS AND TWIRLS IN
    EXCITING
PATTERNS MARRIAGE UNITES OUR LOVE AND TRUST
INHALE THE LUSICIOUS SCENT OF EARTH'S MYSTERY
FOR THIS CAN BE THE SALVATION AND BEGINNING OF
    OUR
ETERNAL VOWS
YOUR PRESCENCE MELTS MY HEART WITH PASSIONATE
    FLAMES
THIS DAY IS OUR DREAM MAY IT ALWAYS BE OUR'S
    FOREVER

Status Equals Nothing

In the laboratory of truth, can the mind be corrupted
Under the microscope societies appetite for pleasure
Before justice can render unconditional surrender
Of morality
Spiritualy bankrupt, Monaterily hungry
Objects of no consequence become status
A new millineum has dawned
Now the importance for redirection of attitudes
And platitudes comes into play
High price status symbols should no longer
Measure one's worth
To give is better than to get humanity to each
Ocher "rules"

Stop and See

We as a society work so hard by the hour
to quench our thirst for unlimited power
take time out to smell a rose
and try to describe that feeling in prose
rewards cannot be measured by wealth
but putting it simply, it's more important to
have good health
the best things in life are free
so why not take a chance and see
slow down your hectic pace
and gratefully enjoy the human race

Sudden Shock

He left this morning kissed my cheek
Said he'll be back in a week
While in his car sun shining day
A drunk driver passed a red light
The rules he didn't obey
At ten o'clock the phone rang
Loud and dear, seeming to make
Sure I certainly would hear
He was my lover, friend, husband
He was my pride and joy
He was so elated at the birth
Of our newborn baby boy
What can one say when there
Are no words
Stunned motionless shock every
Breath noisy like a ticking clock
Time may tell if I'll heal from
Being apart
No thread will ever mend my broken heart

Summer Pests

"Ah" Summer heat and humidity, time for delectable dining
The pesty mosquito surveys their helpless tasty morsel victims
We humans should carry signs on our clothing stating
"No biting or dining after 5pm"
I surmize these flying pests like to approach when one is in the
Throws of enjoyment
Romantic feelings surely cease as cursing, slapping and scratching
Overwhelmes bring forth the repellent spray!
Ah summer, whats left
Sharks using human limbs for a barbecue, bees stinging mosquito's
Spreading the deadly west nile virus
The dentist's chair is suddenly becoming alot more inticing

Sympathy for Sad Times

WHY DO WE UTTER SPONTANEOUSLY: HOW OLD
WERE THEY
WHEN A LOVED ONE PASSES AWAY?
DOES THE AGE AT ONE'S DEATH DIMINISH IT'S
IMPORTANCE?
PEOPLE SAY ENOUGH TIME HAS PASSED FOR THE HURT
TO SUBSIDE
BUT EMOTIONS RUN STRONG, AND ARE NOT EASY TO
HIDE
TO GRIEVE IS PART OF LIFE
SO HOLD DEAR OUR LOVED ONE IN THIS TIME OF
STRIFE

Take Two Sips

Take two sips of tea
Imagine the majesty of and old oak tree
Take two sips of tea
It's time out for a lazy lounge on a sandy island beach
Take two sips of tea
Negotiate amiably a mega business deal
Take a breather have two sips of tea
Tune into each sound of music's passionate interpretation
Take two sips of tea
Savor the flavor while planning an anniversary surprise
Steep a pot of herbal tea
Later with mind skill and ingenuity devise a new basis
For man's social, moral interaction with each other and
"TAKE TWO SIPS OF TEA"

Tax Time Again

THE MONTH OF APRIL
TAX TIME FAX TIME
RUSHING TO PUT THINGS IN ORDER
OR SHOULD I HEAD FOR THE BORDER
DEALING WITH THE I.R.S.
IS LIKE A SESSION WITH
"ELLIOT NESS"
HAVE TO COPE WITH IT
WILL I HAVE PATIENCE
TO SIT UNTIL ALL IS DONE
HOPE TO COMPLETE, BEFORE
THE NEXT RISE OF SUN

Tears

THERE ARE TEARS OF HAPPINESS
THERE ARE TEARS OF JOY
TEARS ALSO FALL WITH THE ARRIVAL OF A BABY BOYY
TEARS COLLECT ON OUR FACES
TEARS THAT CANNOT HIDE SORROWS TRACES
TEARS ARE SO MUCH LIKE RAIN
MOIST AND SWEET LIKE CANDY CANE
FALLING FROM OUR EYES LIKE A WET CHAIN
IN CONCLUSION ONE CAN SAY
TEARS DONT ALWAYS MEAN SADNESS
SOMETIMES TEARS SIGNIFY SINCERE GLADNESS

Teller of Taless

WHAT IS A WRITER
A RACONTEUR, TELLER OF TALES
WITH TENACITY AND KEEN INSTINCTS THE STORIES
WILL EVOLVE AND RESOLVE
TALES OF WOMEN IN HISTORY
WITH DARK MYSTERIOUS VEILS
SOME PIRATE SHIPS WITH BLACK SKULL SALS
RAINY DAY HARD SHELLED SNAILS
SUMMER RECORD HEAT
CHILDREN AT THE BEACH
CARRYING THEIR SHOVEL AND PAIL
REPORTER WITH GRAY SUIT
PAD IN HAND, TOUGH AS NAILS
GHETTO SHOOTING SET BAIL
FOR JUVENILE SUSPECT IN JAIL
WEATHER REPORTER, WATCH OUT
FOR HURRICANE NICKNAMED GAIL
A RESCUEAT SEA DUE TO PLANE DISASTER
MUST PUT BEST EFFORT, NO TIME TO FAIL
BELOVED PRINCESS KILLED!
YES IT WAS DIANA
PRINCESS OF WALES
AS LONG AS EACH DAY TURNS TO NIGHT
THERE WILL ALWAYS BE STORIES
FOR MONETARY SALE TO WRITE

The Carrot and the Celery Stalk

SET UPON A MARBLE TABLE IN A FANCY
RESTAURANT SITS A SLVER BOWL SO DREAMY IN IT
ARE ASSORTED COLD VEGETABLES NOT HOT AND
    STEAMY
AMONG THIS ASSORTMENT OF VARYING SIZES AND
    SHAPES
WERE RED CHERRY TOMATOES, SLIM CELERY STALKS
ORANGE CARROT STICKS AND PURPLE SEEDLESS
    GRAPES
WITH EACH NEW CROWD AND DAY PATRONS WOULD
ADMIRE THE BOWL AND SAY
"WHICH SHOULD I PARTAKE OF FIRST, THE BRIGHT
    ORANGE
CARROT STICK OR THE PALE CELERY STALK"
ALWAYS THE FIRST CHOICE WERE THE SHINY ROUND
    GRAPES
FOR A LONG PERIOD OF TIME THINGS REMAINED
    STATUS QUO
UNTIL A PARTY OF SIX ARRIVED WANTING CANDLES
    ON THEIR
BIRTHDAY CAKE TO BLOW
THE STAFF SEARCHED FROM BOTTOM TO TOP
NO CANDLES POTENTIAL PARTY FLOP
ALL OF A SUDDEN SOMEONE SAID "WHY NOT USE THE
CELERY STALKS AND CARROT STICKS INSTEAD"
SO BEGAN A NEW IDEA ENJOYED BY ALL
BEING ABLE TO LIGHT AND EAT THE CANDLES AND
    HAVE A PARTY BALL

The Color of Love

THE COLOR OF LOVE TRANSCENDS DESCRIPTION
FOR WHAT DOES ONE SEE IN THE LOVE PRESCRIPTION
SLEEPLESS NIGHTS
HURTFUL FIGHTS
STOMACH CHURNING
DESIRES BURNING
PALE MOONS. BEAUTIFUL TUNES
STARS SHINING, MIDNIGHT DINING
NEVER LET ANYONE DIMINISH YOUR TRUE FEELINGS
THE WONDERS OF LOVE CAN SET YOUR MIND AND
        BODY REELING

The Daze of Summer

Each summers day as I try to unwind
I begin to envision photographs in a section
of my mind
And I reflect upon my ties that bind
My children pulling me every which way
Saying hurry up I want to go out and play
Husband with leather briefcase in hand
Looking for a new account to land
The hot summer breeze barely moving the trees
Bright yellow marigolds, and buzzing bumble bees
The beach with blue waves and sand castles
Small children fighting parent battles
The sweltering humidity and heat
The hum of the air conditioner blowing at my feet
People anxiously waiting for vacation
To relieve the boredom of the subway
station
Come September the summer will be over and if I find a four leaf clover
I'll dream about the "White Cliffs of Dover

The Dreaded Call

One by one they file in
Neither male or female within this group with a smile or grin
Each holding a summons for jury duty to report
Citizens musing can there be a retort?
Equipped with newspaper, books, laptop computers
An edginess that allows no patience
These men and women representing a wide diversity for a jury pool
When selected must obey the golden rule
Names are announced without rhyme or reason
You'll surely be excused if you advocate treason
At last the day is over each person not selected will have to return
Grumbling and eyes doing a slow burn
Luckily for me I'm a chosen one
I'll miss a few days of work out in the hot sun
During my lunch break I'll eat my hotdog on a bun
Hopefully when the trial is over and my civic duty is complete
My everyday life will have a new meaning as I return to my job
As a engineer which I enjoy whether out in the sun or sleet

The Power of Words

THE POWER OF WORDS
WHETHER WRITTEN OR SPOKEN
SHOULD NOT BE IDLE RHETORIC
FOR FEELINGS AND PROMISES BROKEN
WORDS, SUCH AS HATE, VIOLENCE, AND LOVE
CAN FORM AND FIT INTO A FRAME
LIKE A HAND IN A GLOVE
A SPOKEN OR WRITTEN WORD CAN CHANGE YOUR LIFE
FROM JOY AND HAPPINESS TO SAD FEELNGS
THAT CUT THROUGH THE HEART LIKE A KNIFE
IMAGINE THE WARS AND DESTRUCTION THAT BEGAN
WHEN SIGNING ON THE DOTTED LINE WITH A PEN
LOOK AT THE HORRIFIC RESULTS FROM A PURCHASE
    RECEIPT
FOR EXPLOSIVE DEVICES THAT KILL AND MAIM
    CAUSING HAVOC
IN THE STREET
WORDS MEAN SO MUCH
THEY COMFORT AS MUCH AS A GENTLE TOUCH
BE AWARE, CHOOSE TO WRITE OR SPEAK WORDS WITH
    CARE
THAT WHEN SPOKEN OR WRITTEN PEOPLE WILL WANT
    TO HEAR

The Room

In the dark and dusty gloom
I retreat to the solace of the room
should I allow the sun to shine in
I say to myself with a grin
Bright picturesque paintings adorn the wall
this room is mine even though small
No one can receive so much pleasure
as myself, when I retire to my room during my leisure
Maybe a poem or a symphony I'll ponder
aside from my family with whom I feel the strongest bond
the room is the place where I create without a magic wand
sometimes even as I sleep, ideas begin to fester fast
Into the room I run so my ideas will last
everyone should have that special place
so ingenuity won't go to waste

The Silver Tilted Windmill

As I DRIVE PAST
THE SILVER TILTED WINDMILL EVERYDAY
SAME ONE AS CHILDREN YOU AND I
WOULD TRY TO CLIMB INSIDE TO PLAY
LOWER ON THE LEFT SIDE-TILTED TO THE RIGHT
I WONDER IF THE OLD SPOKES STILL
SHINE UNDER THE STARS AT NIGHT
STILL A MAGIC SIGHT TO SEE
BEAUTIFULLY MAJESTIC IN ITS ENORMITY
NO MATTER HOW MANY YEARS WE'VE BEEN
MARRIED AND ALWAYS TO EACH OTHER
TRUE BLUE
THE SILVER TILTED WINDMILL WILL FOREVER
INVOKE WONDERFUL MEMORIES THAT BIND
US LIKE GLUE

The Trial Awaits

SITTING IN A COURTROOM ON TRIAL FOR HIS LIFE
THIS DEFENDANT WAS ACCUSED OF MURDERING HIS
    WIFE
WITH SO MUCH AT STAKE
THINKING ABOUT HIS TRIAL MADE HIS LEGS SHAKE
HOW DID ALL THIS COME TO BE?
A STORY UNFOLDS: WAIT AND SEE
PERHAPS HE LOVED HER TO MUCH, NOTHING COULD
    COME
BETWEEN
AS THE YEARS PASSED, HER LOVE FOR HIM
CAME APART AT THE SEAM
JEALOUSY AND DOUBTING, FACIAL POUT, VERBAL
    SHOUTING
TILL ONE DAY IT WAS ALL TO MUCH
HE REALIZED, NO LONGER WOULD HE SHARE HER
    GENTLE TOUCH
HE REFLECTED, FELT REJECTED
ONE FATEFUL DAY WHILE SHE LAY BESIDE HIM FAST
    ASLEEP
HE PONDERED, DECIDING THERE WAS NO OTHER WAY
NOTHING LEFT TO SAY
PREPARINGA COFFEE CUP LACED WITH A FATALPOTION
WHEN TASTED, WOULD FOREVER CEASE HER MOTION
SUDDENLYI WAS JOLTED BY A SLIGHT NUDGE
I HAD BEEN DREAMING, JUST COULDN'T BUDGE
LOOKING OVER, MY MATE I DID SEE
HER CURIOUS EYES STARING AT ME

The Twists of Nature

Fever pirched chorography, ballet
Swirling tango, twisted gray spiral coming closer
Bass throated roar, barely audible
A vision, both magnificent, and ferocious
The brain can hardly comprehend
A millisecond in reality
Time stands immobile, as nature
Unleashes it's rath upon the unsuspecting
Property, called home destroyed like
Pick up. sticks, Trees uprooted, Boats, Trucks
And automobiles tossed about like a salad
Drama unfolding-Baited breath
No prophet can predict, the next occurrence
Man can later rebuild from this fury
Human life thrust to their endurance limit
We must have forgiveness, although never forget
Only a higher being knows the reason

The Wonderful World of Technology

DIGITAL TECHNOLOGY IS THE WAY TO GO
WHETHER YOUR A NOVICE OR PRO
A VAST EMPIRE OF KNOWLEDGE IS AT YOUR FINGER
    TIPS
JUST SPREAD THE WORD FROM YOUR LIPs
TIRED OF RECEIVING YOUR LETTERS AS SLOW AS A
    SNAIL
SIGN ON FOR ELECITRIC E-MAIL
COMPUTER IMAGING THAT CAN CHANGE YOUR
    CLOTHING LOOK
YOU CAN THROW AWAY THE CATALOG BOOK
NO MORE HUNTING FOR JOBS WHILE YOU ROAM
GET A COMPUTER, YOULL EARN AS YOU LEARN FROM
    HOME
FROM C-D ROM TO THE DYNAMIC INTERNET
YOULL BE AMAZED AT ALL YOU GET
JUST BE ALERT, DONT FEEL WEARY
EVEN THOUGH FUTURE TECHNOLOGYIS SOMETIMES
    SCARY

35 Would Be Nice

Thirty five would be nice
So much left of life's spice
Not ready or willing to punch the clock
For a senior supper of dry rice
Thirty five would be nice
Toasting marshmallows at a fire place, cozy
And warm after a downhill ski slope race
Children and grandkids nothing can compare
Sometimes unable to remove desire for pulling
Out my hair
Weariness and old bones tell the tale
Reminiscing down life's lane slowly deliberate like a hard shell
snail
Each of us has their own story to unfold and
A certain ages everything went well
Thirty five would be nice you see
But I now cherish each day with glee

Topics

THERE ARE SEVEN DAYS IN A WEEK
THERE ARE 365 DAYS TO A YEAR
THERE ARE FOUR SEASONS, AND THERE ARE
  NUMEROUS REASONS
REASONS GIVEN FOR BEING UNKND
REASONS FOR THE SPECIAL WAY THE PLANETS ARE
  ALIGNED
THERE IS REASON TO HOPE, AND LIVNG THINGSTO DIE
SOME
TIMES WE SEEK ANSWERS, BUT SELDOM ARE THEY
  FOUND
OCEANS WILL LIVE FOREVER
SEASONS WILL CHANGE
BUT THE MAGICAL MYSTERY OF LIFES "LUCK OF THE
  DRAW"
CAN NEVER BE EXPLAINED

Transformation of Lola

She gives the appearance of a child
Petite body innocence in abundance
Tousled blond mane of short hair
The most expressive liquid green eyes
Juvenile smiling rouge red lips
Winter clothing hides the secrets, arms covered by long sleeves
With the first hint of warmer weather out comes the box
Inside are tank tops, solid, striped, even ones with polka dots
Once attired in these her secret can no longer be kept
Adorning her pale skinned arms are the "tattoos"
Conversation topics all Hindu writing when translated means
Shameless One
A red rose with droplets of tears
Multicolored butterfly the third one so far
Perhaps each person harbors inner thoughts and desires
Many would never act upon
Lola is a chameleon always keeping her agenda a mystery
Friends envy her spirit and willingness to take the risks
Society frowns upon those who choose adornments
It isn't the exterior of the person but the courage and spunk
Tattoos don't equal toughness Lola is gifted with a gentle soul
Lola is cool and sassy she brings the sun wherever she goes

Tranquility

One morning while the streaks from the sunshine
Draw my attention to the kitchen window I watch
As the waves from the beach gently ebb heir way
To the shore and back I take a break to breathe
Soon the day changes to night and the full moon
Glistens on the tranquil water
I reflect upon the calmness of my demeanor
I wish that I could remain this placid when morning
Sun does arrive again, but as a new day dawns
The reality of life looms heavy in my heart due
To the lack of feelings and caring of all humanity
Why can't society join in dignity for all

Twin Tower

It took only an instant and the destruction began
So much like the tragedy of 103 Pan Am
The earth shook and the smoke spewed like a shout
People inside were so anxious to get out
Who would believe such an absurdity could happen
Here, it just proves nothing is safe anywhere
So many hero's from police to firemen, to ems
But the people themselves rose to this tragedy
The best!
It will take patience and time to place the blame
And those responsible should recoil with shame
The children who witnessed this will have plenty
To say these horrific memories will haunt them
Even at play
Inspite of all this the TWIN TOWER'S can no
Longer stand tall as do tree's
And we can show the world that new yorker's
Can't and won't be brought to their knee's

Vanilla

Aromatic Vanilla made from the bean
Lingering sweet fragrance somewhere inbetween
The moon, the milky way and a shimmering rainbow sunbeam
Delicious ingredient for french vanilla ice-cream
Walking outside in the rain under my umbrella
Deep in thought about my date with a new fella
Rain drops in the puddles imagination galore made me
Hurry to a nearby bakery store
Once inside requesting the best scone of vanilla
Munching brings my palate thoughts so stellar
Bag of goodies in my hand my feet move to a melodic
Tarantella next I'm off to my date with a lucky fella

Visitors Paradise

THERE IS A PLACE WITH AN ABUNDANCE OF SPACE
CALLED THE
"GRAND CANYON"
WITH MAJESTIC MOUNTAINS SO SERENE
CAPPED ON TOP WITH WHITE LIKE MOUNDS THAT
RESEMBLE
WHIPPED CREAM
THIS MAGNIFICENT LANDSCAPE SO ABUNDANT WITH
DIFFERENT HUES
LIKE THE ARTIST'S PALETTE LADEN WITH DIFFERENT
SHADES OF BLUE
LIVING IN THIS WONDROUS PRODUCT OF NATURE
ARE ANIMALS OF DIFFERENT SPECIES
FLOWERS OF IMPRESSIVE COLORS ARE NURTURED BY
THE GOLDEN SUN
MUSICAL SOUNDS REBOUND OFF THE MOUNTAINS
ECHOING THEIR LYRICAL TONES
PERHAPS THERE MAY ALSO BE DECAYING ANIMAL
BONES
SUCH AN EXTRAORDINARY PLACE WHERE VISITORS
COME LOADED
WITH CAMERA'S AND CAMCORDERS
TO CAPTURE THE EXQUISITE BEAUTY AND WONDERS
OF THE EARTH
CAUSING REFLECTIVE THOUGHTS ABOUT LIFE, DEATH,
AND THE MIRACLE
OF BIRTH

Wedding Thoughts

Sleep doesn't happen easily for me tonight
Tree branches take their places on the dew
soaked ground
Moon in crescent form illuminates the evening
sky
I'm worn out by weighty thoughts upon my
Tired brain
The ticking sound of the clock on my night
Table awakens reality with each minute
Elation, panic, uncertainty, all causing my
Heart to pound inside my chest
When the sun rises in the morning changes
From me to us will rule
The man that means everything to me becomes
My husband
A transition I have wanted for a long time

When the Bough Breaks

Tree's have limbs with arms outstretched
Standing tall for all to see
Cut them down and tears might fall even though
It's just a tree
The boughs of humanity have reached perilous
Proportions stressing the limit of sanity
Recent events will forever alter the status quo
Children's eyes once bright are sorrow filled by vacate Stares
Hysteria for diseases hoped eradicated and distant
Life is like a branch hanging in the wind
Society can ill afford to be indifferent
Where have all the flowers gone?
Our boughs must remain intact through these difficult
Days and years ahead
The human race must be able to answer
Where have all the flowers gone

Why I Write

The mime does his elaborate hand and body gestures
To display the thoughts and feelings
The artist with palette and brush and specific images
Conveys his ideas through color and brings to life
His essay on canvas to completion
The poet with accompaning parts of speech serves
Up turmoil, affection, illness, religion, emotions
Stories and can thus entertain and educate
Preferring to remain voiceless with sound
But expressive with words is why I write

A Wonder of Nature

WELCOME PEOPLE TO THE LAND OF THE FREE
AND THE HOME OF THE BRAVE
WHERE YOUR MIND AND BODY CAN EXPLORE
THE BEAUTIFUL "GRAND CANYON", WITH IT'S
DARK CAVES, EXQUISTTE SIGHTS, MULITTUDENOUS
WONDERs, ALONG WITH IT'S DANGER
CANNOT DETER THE THOUSANDS OF VISITING
STRANGERS
MEN, WOMAN, CHILDREN AND THE LIKE
COME THERE TO EXPLORE AND TO HIKE
ONCE SEEN THE MIND CAN WANDER FREE
IN AWE OF ALL THERE IS TO SEE
SO IF YOUR PLANNING A VACATION
LEAVE BEHIND THE BLAND AND BE SURE
YOUR VISIT TO THE "GRAND CANYON"
WILL BE THE PLACE YOU ADORE